KNITTING
Children's Sweaters

© 1992 Lyric Books Ltd
PO Box 152, Mill Hill, London NW7, England

First published in 1992

ISBN 0 7111 0015 2

Printed in Belgium by
Proost International Book Production

Introduction

HARMONY CLASS is for everyone. Beginners will find it friendly and instructional, experienced knitters will find it challenging and informative.

Step-by-step instructions for some of the most common techniques for working with colour are followed by knitting instructions for a classic stocking stitch Sweater.

The classic Sweater is the basis for all the design variations that can be made by working the stitches or Intarsia patterns. The third section suggests a few of the many ways you can create an individual garment using the stitches and designs to inspire you, but remember - **the choice is yours**.

Basic knitting techniques which will be of particular interest to the less experienced knitter follow, and we finish with some hints and tips which could be helpful to all of you.

Incidentally, we would be glad to hear from you if you have tips which we can add to future editions of our books and which would interest other knitters.

Contents

Knitting with Colour

The introduction of colour in knitting is one of the simplest ways to add interest and variety to an otherwise plain garment. Colour can be introduced in several ways, from very simple stripe and colour block patterns to intricate Intarsia and Fairisle work. While stripes and Intarsia (or colour block) patterns can be added to any plain stocking stitch garment, Fairisle patterns will change the tension of the fabric and therefore the pattern instructions would have to be amended.

This book concentrates on ways of adding colour to a children's classic stocking stitch sweater, without having to amend the instructions. In addition, colour can also be added in the form of surface embroidery or fabric appliqué. The possibilities are endless, and with a little imagination you can create your own individual Designer Sweater!

Horizontal Stripes

This is the easiest way of adding colour to a basic garment. You work the required number of rows in one colour, then drop the yarn and pick up the next colour. To ensure that the new colour is laying at the right end of the row so that it doesn't have to be cut each time you change colour, work an even number of rows if you are using two colours or an odd number of rows if you are using three colours. To keep the edge of the work neat the yarn can be carried **loosely** up the side of the work, without cutting it off at each colour change. If the stripes are fairly deep cross the yarns over at the beginning of alternate rows, to avoid long loops between the stripes.

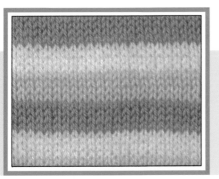

Intarsia

Intarsia is the name given to colour knitting where the pattern is worked in large colour blocks, or over large areas at a time, requiring separate balls or lengths of yarn to be used for each area of colour. There can be any number of colours across a row, but because of the size of each patch of colour the spare yarns should **not** be stranded across the back of the work. Generally Intarsia knitting is worked in stocking stitch (although it can be worked in any textured pattern) and is used for large geometric patterns, patchworks, picture knitting or individual motifs.

Twisting Yarns Together
Vertical line

When the colour change is in a vertical line, on a right side row work to the colour change, then making sure both yarns are at the back of the work, drop the first colour, pick up the second colour and bring it around the first colour to cross the yarns over before working the next stitch. On a wrong side row, make sure both yarns are at the front (wrong side) of the work. Drop the first colour, pick up the second colour and bring it around the first colour before working the next

Because of the scale of the designs, patterns are usually given in chart form - sometimes a complete section of a garment is shown if the pattern is large and non-repetitive.

Intarsia or motif knitting can produce beautiful results if worked correctly. Because you will be working with several separate lengths of yarn, there may be a number of ends to be sewn in once the garment is completed. Do not carry yarns across large areas or weave the colours in as the results will always be disappointing, and the tension may be altered.

It is important when working Intarsia to always twist the two yarns together when you change colour, otherwise you will be creating completely separate pieces of knitting! The yarns must be twisted over each other to link them and prevent a hole forming between the colours. Always cross the yarns over on the **wrong side** of the work.

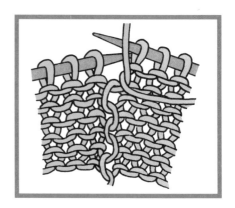

stitch. This technique ensures that the yarns are crossed on every row, and gives a neat, unbroken vertical line on the right side. Work the first stitch in each colour firmly to avoid a gap forming between the colours.

Diagonal slant to the right

When the colour change slants to the right, the yarns are crossed on a right side row. Take the first colour in front of the second colour, drop it, then pick

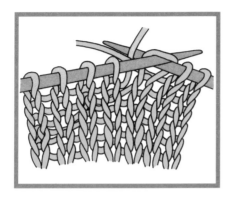

before securing, otherwise the stitch will appear loose on the right side. The ends can be run along the line of the colour change on the wrong side as this will be less visible on the right side.

The photographs below illustrate a combination of vertical and diagonal colour changes from the wrong and right side of the work.

up the second colour and work with it, thus twisting the two colours together. On a wrong side row the yarns will cross automatically because of the direction of the diagonal slant.

Diagonal slant to the left

When the diagonal slants to the left, the yarns are crossed on a wrong side row as shown. On a right side row the yarns cross automatically.

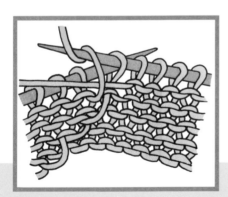

With any Intarsia pattern, leave a long end of yarn at the start and finish of each area of colour - as they are within the work it is important to secure them carefully. Draw the end up firmly

Using Bobbins

Where two or more colours are used in a row, or when the same colour is used in a number of places, it can be difficult to avoid tangling the yarn. Using bobbins keeps the yarns separate by allowing them to hang at the back of the work until they are needed. They are ideal for motif knitting where only a small length of yarn is required.

Plastic bobbins are obtainable from most knitting shops, but you can make your own out of stiff card. Ensure that the slit at the top holds the yarn end securely and allows you to unwind a controlled amount of yarn at a time. Use a separate bobbin for each block of colour, winding on sufficient yarn to complete an entire area if possible.

Working from a Chart

Knitting instructions for Intarsia and Fairisle patterns are usually given in chart form. Either the complete design or a single pattern repeat of it (which must be worked across the width and depth of the fabric) is shown as a chart on a grid. The colours in the pattern are either represented by symbols that are identified in an adjacent key, or the squares are shaded in the relevant colour.

Reading a chart is easier if you visualise it as a piece of knitting working from the lower edge to the top. Horizontally across the grid each square represents a stitch and vertically up the grid each square represents a row of knitting.

The details of how to follow a chart are usually given with the pattern but generally the following rules apply.

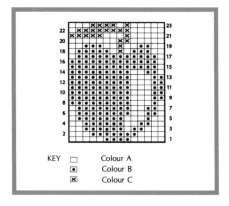

KEY □ Colour A
     ⊡ Colour B
     ☒ Colour C

Rows: For stocking stitch, work across a line of squares reading from right to left for the knit rows, then follow the line immediately above reading from left to right for the purl rows. Odd numbers at the right-hand edge usually indicate the knit rows, while even numbers at the left-hand edge denote the purl rows. To make following a chart easier, use a row counter and place a ruler under the row being worked and move the ruler up as each row is completed.

Stitches: If only one repeat of the pattern is given in the chart, this has to be repeated across the width of the material. This section is usually contained within bold vertical lines with a bracketed indication that it is to be repeated across the row. There may be extra stitches at either end which are edge stitches worked at the beginning and end of rows to complete the pattern so that the rows are symmetrical or 'balanced'.

For motif knitting, the chart is worked between slip markers (see page 41) over a given number of stitches.

Embroidery on Knitting

Stocking stitch garments make an ideal surface for embroidery but it is easier to work before the garment is sewn together. Use a large, blunt-ended needle and a yarn of a similar thickness.

Swiss Darning or Duplicate Stitch

This is a form of embroidery on knitting that duplicates the knitted stitches so that it looks as if the design has been knitted in. This useful and versatile technique, besides being added to a plain stocking stitch fabric, can be included in Fairisle or Intarsia patterns where very small or widely spaced motifs are difficult to add during the knitting process. Always work to a similar tension to the knitting - too loose and the stitches will not be covered, too tight and the work will pucker. If the yarn is finer than the knitted yarn it may not cover the knitted stitch completely.

Swiss darning vertically

Work from bottom to top. Weave in the embroidery yarn invisibly at the back of the work. Bring the needle out at the base of the first stitch, then take it around the top of the stitch under the stitch above. Insert the needle back through the base of the **same** stitch then up through the base of the stitch above, thus forming a vertical chain.

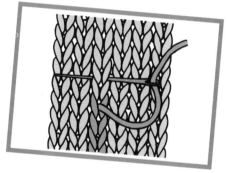

Swiss darning horizontally

Work from right to left. Bring the needle out at the base of the first stitch,

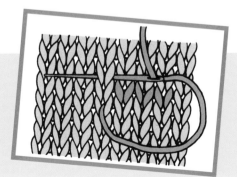

take it around the top of the stitch under the stitch above, then insert the needle back through the base of the **same** stitch, thus covering the original stitch completely. Bring the needle through at the base of the next stitch to the left and continue in this way until the required area is covered.

Embroidery Stitches

Designs can be simple in just one stitch, or they can be more elaborate using a combination of the stitches in several colours. To keep the embroidery neat and uniform use the stitches and rows of knitting as a guide to size.

French Knot

Bring the needle from the back to the front of the work and wind the yarn several times around the needle according to the size of knot required. Take the needle back through the

same place and draw the yarn through, thus forming a small knot on the right side. If the knot tends to slip

through to the wrong side, insert the needle half a stitch further on to avoid this.

Cross Stitch

Work across one or two stitches and rows as required, inserting the needle between the stitches to avoid splitting the yarn.

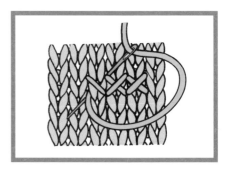

Stem Stitch

This is a continuous line of long stitches, worked from left to right in a similar way to backstitch, but each stitch overlaps the previous one by half its length (as on the **wrong** side of back stitch).

Pattern and Designs

Child's Round Neck Sweater

To Fit

Chest sizes	55	60	65	70	cm
	22	24	26	28	ins
Finished measurement	68	74	79	84	cm
	27	29$^1/_2$	31$^1/_2$	33	ins
Length to shoulder	39	43	46	50	cm
	15$^1/_2$	17	18	19$^1/_2$	ins
Sleeve length	25	29	33	36	cm
	10	11$^1/_2$	13	14	ins

Materials

Double Knitting	300	325	375	425	grams
(see page 48 for yarn equivalents)					approx.

Pair needles each size 4mm (No 8) and 3mm (No 10).

Tension

22 sts and 30 rows = 10 cm [4 ins] square measured over st st using larger needles. See tension on page 44.

For notes and abbreviation see page 42.

The quantities of yarn stated are based on average requirements and are therefore approximate.

Back

Using smaller needles cast on 61(67-71-77) sts.

1st row (right side): K1, *p1, k1; rep from * to end.
2nd row: P1, *k1, p1; rep from * to end.

Rep the last 2 rows until rib measures 5(5-6-6) cm [2(2-2$^1/_2$-2$^1/_2$) ins] ending with a right side row.

Next row (increase): Rib 4(7-5-8), *inc in next st, rib 3; rep from * to last 5(8-6-9) sts, inc in next st, rib to end. 75(81-87-93) sts.

Change to larger needles and work in st st, starting knit, until back measures 39(43-46-50) cm [15$^1/_2$(17-18-19$^1/_2$) ins], or required length to shoulders ending with a purl row.

Cast off 26(28-29-31) sts at beg of next 2 rows. Slip remaining 23(25-29-31) sts on to a holder for neckband.

Front

Work as given for Back until front is 17(19-21-23) rows shorter than back to start of shoulder shaping, thus ending with a knit row.

Shape Neck

Next row: P31(34-37-39), turn and complete this side first.

Dec 1 st at neck edge on next 3(3-5-5) rows, then following 2(3-3-3) alt rows. 26(28-29-31) sts remain. Work 10(10-10-12) rows straight, thus ending at side edge. Cast off.

Slip next 13(13-13-15) sts at centre on to a holder. With wrong side facing rejoin yarn to neck edge of remaining 31(34-37-39) sts and purl to end.

Dec 1 st at neck edge on next 3(3-5-5) rows, then following 2(3-3-3) alt rows. 26(28-29-31) sts remain. Work 9(9-9-11) rows straight, thus ending at side edge. Cast off.

Sleeves

Using smaller needles cast on 37(39-41-43) sts and work 5 cm (2 ins) in k1, p1 rib as given for Back ending with a right side row.

Next row (increase): Rib 4(1-2-3), *inc in next st, rib 3(4-3-3); rep from * to last 5(3-3-4) sts, inc in next st, rib to end. 45(47-51-53) sts.

Change to larger needles and work 4 rows in st st, starting knit. Inc 1 st at each end of next and every following 6th row until there are 61(67-73-79) sts. Work straight until sleeve measures 25(29-33-36) cm [10(11½-13-14) ins], or required length ending with a purl row. Cast off.

Finishing and Neckband

Press pieces according to instructions on ball band. Join left shoulder seam.

Neckband: Using smaller needles and with right side facing, knit across sts on holder at back neck increasing 1 st at centre, pick up and k15(17-18-20) sts down left front slope, knit across sts on holder at front neck and pick up and k15(17-18-20) sts up right front slope. 67(73-79-87) sts.

Starting with a 2nd row work 6(6-8-8) cm [2½(2½-3-3) ins] in k1, p1 rib as given for Back. Slip sts onto a length of yarn.

Join right shoulder seam and ends of neckband. Fold neckband in half to inside and slip-stitch **loosely** in place, allowing for stretch and taking care to catch every stitch. Fold sleeves in half lengthways and mark centre of cast off edge. Sew sleeve to side edge placing centre at shoulder seam. **Note:** Armhole should measure approximately 14(15-17-18) cm [5½(6-6¾-7) ins]. Join side and sleeve seams. Press seams if required.

To make the Classic Sweater pattern more interesting, knit sections in different colours similar to the photograph on page 9.

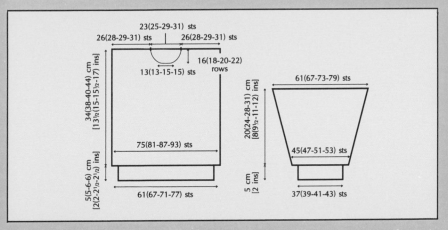

23(25-29-31) sts
26(28-29-31) sts   26(28-29-31) sts
13(13-15-15) sts   16(18-20-22) rows
34(38-40-44) cm [13½(15-15½-17) ins]
75(81-87-93) sts
5(5-6-6) cm [2(2-2½-2½) ins]
61(67-71-77) sts

61(67-73-79) sts
20(24-28-31) cm [8(9½-11-12) ins]
45(47-51-53) sts
5 cm [2 ins]
37(39-41-43) sts

Design Variations

Back and Front

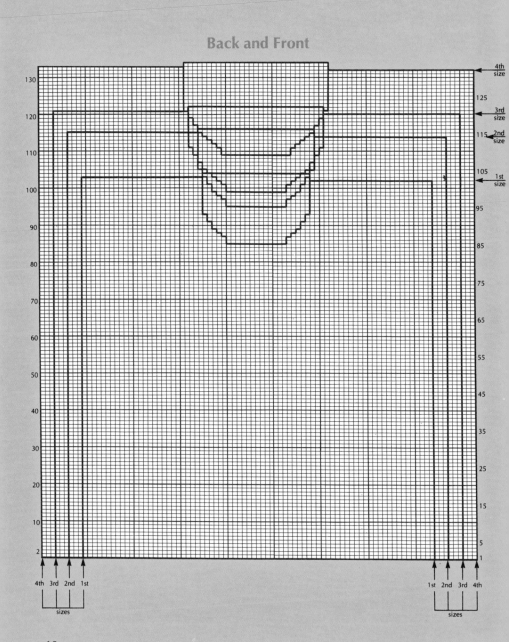

HARMONY CLASS gives you all the information you need to change the classic stocking stitch pattern to any one of the designs shown on the following pages.

A number of the designs are for Intarsia patterns which are given as charts. To make it easier to work these, we have also supplied the classic pattern in chart form. Each square represents one stitch and all the pattern sizes have been shown. You may find it simpler to copy the size you intend to make on to graph paper and then combine it with your chosen Intarsia pattern. Remember, with Intarsia patterns it is often easier to Swiss darn rather than knit small areas.

Any additional information needed to make the individual designs is given with the illustration.

Sleeve

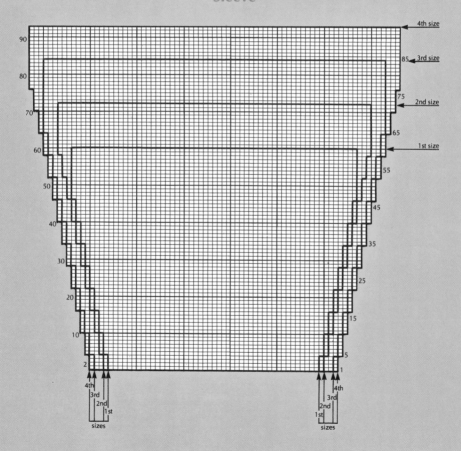

13

Blob Sweater

For the sweater shown we have used a white background and four contrasting colours but you could use any combination or number of colours.

Knit using the size guide chart on pages 12 and 13 for your chosen size, following the colour chart in Intarsia.

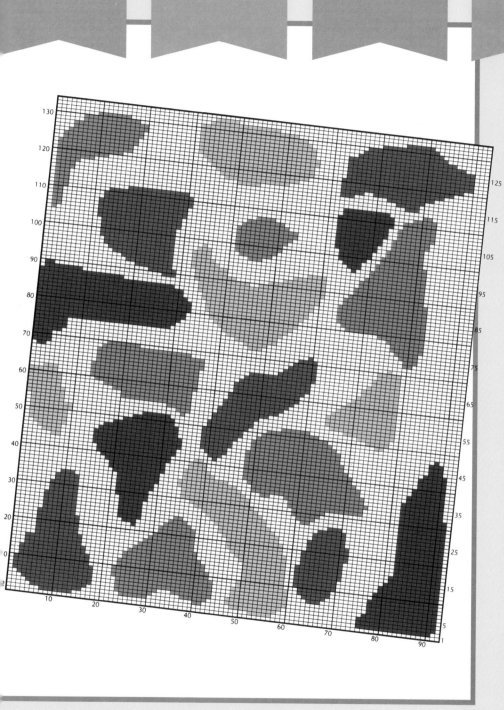

15

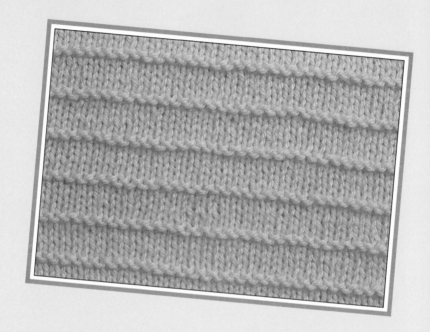

Ridge Stitch Sweater

Any number of stitches.

1st row (right side): Knit.

2nd row: Purl.

Rep these 2 rows once more.

5th and 6th rows: Knit.

Rep these 6 rows.

Any number of sts

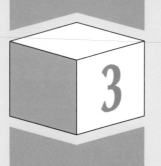

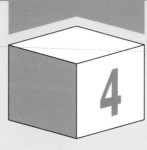

Striped Bee Sweater

Each band of stripes consists of 10 rows: 2 rows each in Yellow and Black alternately.

Front and Back

Work 4(6-10-12) rows in Black, *work 10 rows of stripes, work 30(34-34-38) rows in Black; rep from * to end then work 10 rows of stripes, work 8(10-12-14) rows in Black.

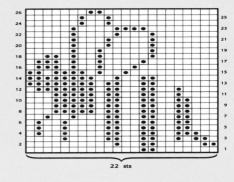

22 sts

Sleeves (work two the same)

Work 6(10-36-34) rows in Black, work 10 rows of stripes.

Work 30(34-34-34) rows in Black, work 10(10-0-10) rows of stripes, work 4(8-0-2) rows in Black.

Once each piece is knitted Swiss darn Bee motifs following chart, between stripes.

Yellow Bee Sweater

Knit sweater plain, then Swiss darn Bee motif, following chart, 3 times across the bottom of the front and back pieces. Place each motif 4 rows up from start a few stitches apart.

5

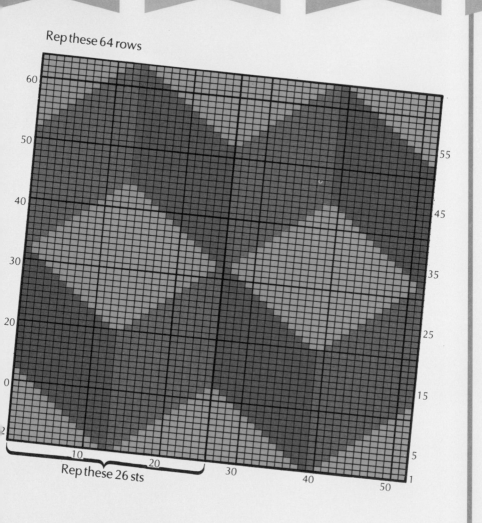

Rep these 64 rows

Rep these 26 sts

Geometric Sweater

Knit body and sleeves in Intarsia following the colour chart. Using the same chart but experimenting with colours you can create a completely different look.

Sunflower Sweater

Knit the body and sleeves in a plain colour.

Front

Following the chart work the basic yellow sunflower shape in Intarsia. Using the size guide chart on pages 12 and 13 plan out the suitable positioning of each motif for your size. After knitting the whole front, randomly embroider French knots in brown yarn in the centre of each motif. Using stem stitch embroider the stems as shown in green yarn.

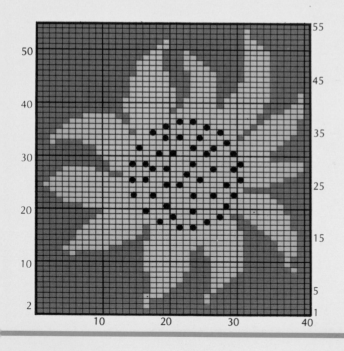

Quartered Sweater

Front and Back

After rib and increase row, work 37(40-43-46) sts in colour A, change to colour B and work the remaining 38(41-44-47) sts.

Continue for 50 rows then change to colour B, work first 37(40-43-46) sts, change to colour A and work the remaining 38(41-44-47) sts, thus reversing the colours.

Sleeves

Knit one sleeve in colour A and one sleeve in colour B. Knit the rib at cuff in the contrasting colour for each sleeve.

Striped Sweater

Knit front, back and sleeves in stripes of 20(23-24-26) rows, the last stripe of each section may have more or less rows. Knit the ribs at waist, neck and cuffs in the contrasting colour as shown.

Fish Sweater

Work the Fish motif in Intarsia on the front of the sweater following the colour chart. Use the size guide chart on pages 12 and 13 to work out the position of the Fish for your chosen size.

Work the sleeves and back plain.

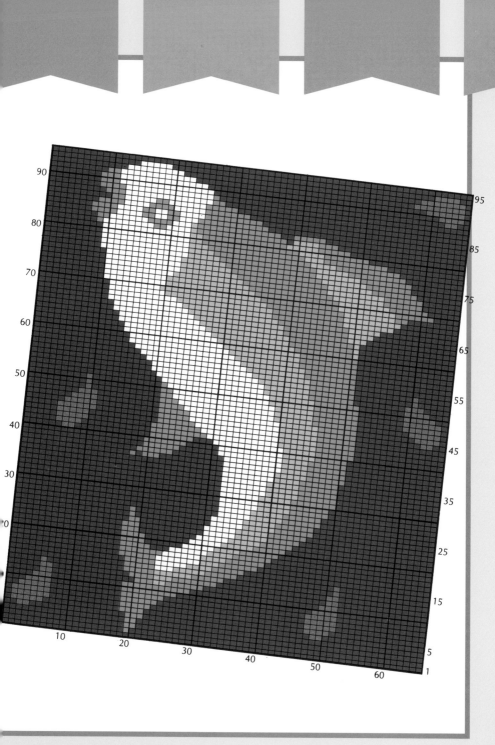

Garter Stitch Ridges

Any number of stitches.

1st row (right side): Knit.

2nd row: Purl.

Rep the last 2 rows once more, then knit 6 rows thus ending with a wrong side row.

Rep these 10 rows.

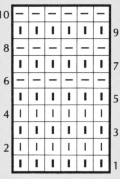

Any number of sts

Striped Garter Stitch Rib Sweater

A = Lilac, B = Dark Blue, C = Purple, D = Light Blue.

1st row (right side): Knit 25(27-29-31)A, 25(27-29-31)B, k to end in A.

2nd row: Purl 25(27-29-31)A, 25(27-29-31)B, p to end in A.

3rd and 4th rows: Rep the last 2 rows once more.

5th row: Knit 25(27-29-31)C, 25(27-29-31)D, k to end in C.

6th to 10th rows: Rep the last row 5 times more.

Rep these 10 rows once more, then repeat the first 4 rows again.

25th row: Knit 25(27-29-31)B, 25(27-29-31)A, k to end in B.

26th to 30th rows: Rep the last row 5 times more.

31st row: Knit 25(27-29-31)D, 25(27-29-31)C, k to end in D.

32nd row: Purl 25(27-29-31)D, 25(27-29-31)C, p to end in D.

33rd and 34th rows: Rep the last 2 rows once more.

Rep from 25th to 34th rows once more, then from 25th to 30th rows once more.

Continue in this way for required number of rows.

Plain Garter Stitch Ridge Sweater

Work sweater following garter stitch ridge pattern in one colour.

Pow Sweater

Front

Using the size guide chart on pages 12 and 13 plan the best position for the POW motif for your size. Work the background of the motif in Intarsia and Swiss darn the word POW! as shown on the colour chart. French knots can then be embroidered randomly in black once each piece is knitted as shown.

Work the back and sleeves plain then embroider random French knots in black on each knitted piece.

Knitting Know How

In the following pages we give detailed instructions and diagrams for working basic stitches, understanding diagrams and working from pattern instructions.

Equipment

Knitting needles are used in pairs to produce a flat knitted fabric. They range in size from 2mm to 17mm in diameter. It is useful to have a range of sizes so that tension swatches can be knitted on various needles and compared. They are also available in various lengths - choose a length that will comfortably hold the stitches required for each project. To produce a tubular fabric or flat rounds (such as circular shawls) use **double-pointed needles** (sold in sets of four or five), or **circular needles** (two needle points joined by a flexible length of plastic).

Cable needles are short double pointed needles used to hold stitches temporarily when knitting cables.

Stitch holders resemble large safety pins and are also used to hold stitches, for example, around a neckline when the neckband stitches will be picked up and worked after the back and front have been joined. Alternatively, thread a contrast-coloured yarn through the stitches to be held while they are on the needle, then slip the stitches off the needle and knot both ends of the contrast yarn together.

Use **blunt pointed needles** for sewing completed pieces of knitting together.

A row counter is a cylinder with a numbered dial that is pushed on to the needle and the dial is turned at the completion of each row.

A tape measure is essential for checking tension swatches and for measuring the length and width of completed knitting.

A crochet hook is useful for picking up dropped stitches.

Knitting Yarn

Yarn is the term used for strands of spun fibre which are twisted into a continuous thread of the required thickness. It can be of animal origin (wool, angora, mohair, silk), vegetable origin (cotton, linen) or man-made (nylon, acrylic, rayon).

Each strand of yarn is known as a ply. A number of plys are twisted together to form the yarn. The texture and characteristics of the yarn may be varied by the combination of fibres and by the way in which it is spun.

Buying Yarn

Yarn manufacturers wrap each ball with a paper band on which is printed a lot of necessary information. The ball band states the weight of the yarn and its composition, gives instructions for washing and ironing and may state the ideal range of needle sizes to be used with the yarn. It also carries the shade number and dye lot number and it is important that you use yarn of the same dye lot for a single project. Different dye lots vary subtly in shading which may not be apparent when you are holding two balls, but which will show as a variation in shade on the finished piece of knitting.

Always keep the ball band as a reference. Pin it to the tension swatch and keep them together with any left over yarn and spare buttons or other trimmings. That way you can always check the washing instructions and also have materials for repairs.

Basic Techniques

Holding the Needles

The right needle is held as if holding a pencil. For casting on and working the first few rows the knitted piece passes over the hand, between the thumb and the index finger. As work progresses let the thumb slide under the knitted piece, grasping the needle from below.

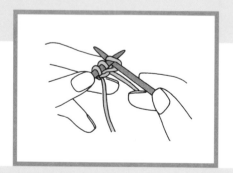

The left needle is held lightly, using the thumb and index finger to control the tip of the needle.

Holding the Yarn

There are various methods of winding the yarn round the fingers to control the tension on the yarn and so produce even knitting. In time you might develop a favourite way but first try the popular method shown here.

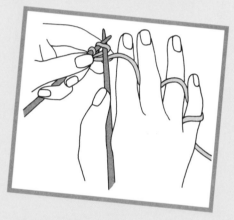

Holding yarn in right hand, pass under the little finger, then around same finger, over third finger, under centre finger and over index finger. The index finger is used to pass the yarn around the needle tip. The yarn circled around the little finger creates the necessary tension for knitting evenly.

Making a Slip Knot

A slip knot is the starting point for almost everything you do in knitting and is the basis of all casting on techniques.

1 Wind the yarn around two fingers and over the two fingers again to the back of the first thread.

Casting On

There are two common methods of casting on. The thumb method is used whenever a very elastic edge is required or when the rows immediately after the cast-on edge are to be worked in garter or stocking stitch. The second method is the cable or 'between stitches' method. This gives a firm neat finish and is best for use before ribbing or any other firm type of stitch.

Thumb Method

1 Make a slip knot about 1m (depending on the number of stitches required) from the end of the yarn. Hold the needle in the right hand with the ball end of the yarn over your first finger. *Wind the loose end of the yarn around the left thumb from front to back.

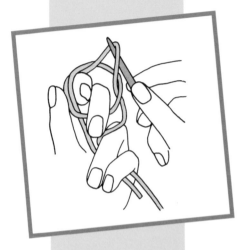

2 Using a knitting needle pull the back thread through the front one to form a loop.

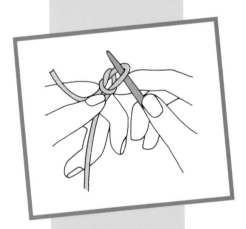

3 Pull end to tighten the loop.

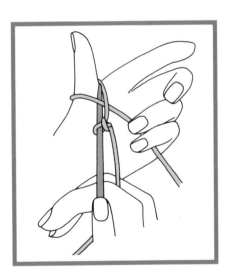

2 Insert the needle through the yarn on the thumb.

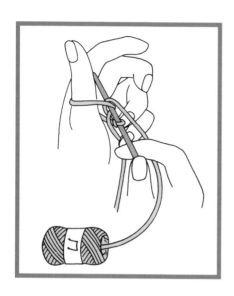

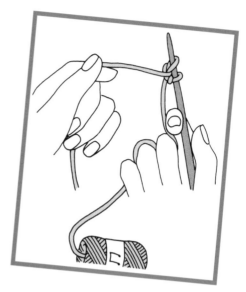

3 Take the ball end of yarn with your right forefinger over the needle point .

5 Remove your left thumb from the yarn and pull the loose end to secure the stitch.

Repeat from * until the required number of stitches has been cast on.

Cable Method

This method requires the use of two needles.

1 Make a slip knot about 10 cm from the end of the yarn.

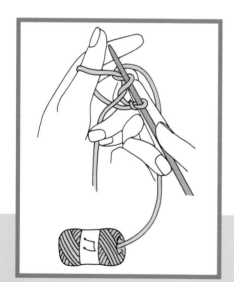

4 Pull a loop through to form the first stitch.

2 Insert right-hand needle through

the loop on left-hand needle and pass the yarn over the right needle.

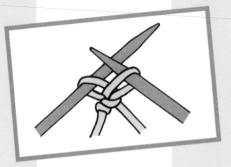

3 Draw a loop through with the right-hand needle.

4 Place this loop on the left-hand needle.

5 Insert right-hand needle between

the two stitches on the left-hand needle. Wind yarn round point of right-hand needle.

6 Draw a loop through, place this loop on left-hand needle.

Repeat steps 5 and 6 until the required number of stitches has been cast on.

The Basic Stitches

Knit Stitches

1 Hold the needle with the cast on stitches in the left hand. With the yarn at back of work, insert the right-hand needle from left to right through the front of the first stitch on left-hand needle.

2 Wind the yarn from left to right over the point of the right-hand needle.

3 Draw the yarn back through the stitch, thus forming a loop on the right-hand needle.

4 Slip the original stitch off the left-hand needle.

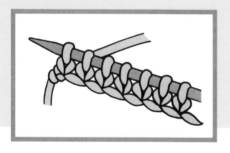

To knit a row, repeat steps 1 to 4 until all the stitches have been transferred from the left needle to the right needle. Turn the work and transfer the needle with the stitches on to the left hand to work the next row.

When every row is knitted (known as garter stitch) both sides of the fabric have raised horizontal ridges.

Purl Stitches

1 With the yarn at the front of the work insert the right-hand needle from right to left through the front of the first stitch on the left-hand needle.

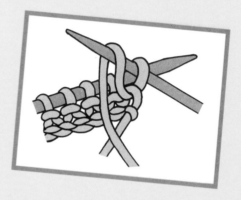

2 Wind the yarn from right to left over the point of the right-hand needle.

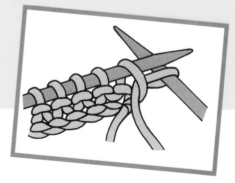

3 Draw a loop through on to the right-hand needle.

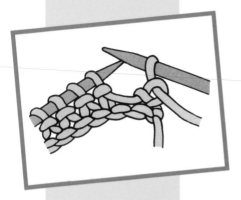

2 Bring the yarn forward to the front of the work between the needles and purl the next stitch.

4 Slip the original stitch off the left-hand needle.

To purl a row, repeat steps 1 to 4 until all the stitches are transferred to the right-hand needle, then turn the work and transfer the needles to work the next row.

Purling every row also gives garter stitch but can be slower to work.

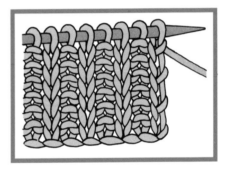

Stocking Stitch (st st)

Stocking stitch is the most widely knitted fabric, comprising of alternate knit and purl rows.

3 Take the yarn to the back of the work between the needles and knit the next stitch.

Repeat steps 2 and 3 until all stitches are transferred to the right-hand needle.

Always ensure that stitches which are knitted on one row are purled on the following row and vice versa.

Single Rib (k1, p1)

This is formed by alternately knitting a stitch, then purling a stitch to give unbroken vertical lines on each side of the work. It is used for borders such as welts, neckbands and cuffs and is generally worked on a smaller size needle than the main body of the garment to keep it firm and elastic.

1 Knit the first stitch.

Casting Off

Always cast off in pattern. This means that in stocking stitch you cast off knit-wise on a knit row and purlwise on a purl row. Casting off ribbing should always be done as if you were continuing to rib. Most pattern stitches can also be followed during the course of the casting off.

Casting Off Knitwise

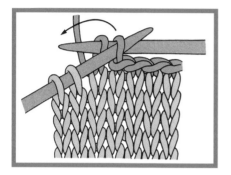

Knit the first two stitches. *Using the left-hand needle lift the first stitch over the second and drop it off the needle. Knit the next stitch and repeat from the * until all the stitches have been worked from the left-hand needle and one stitch only remains on the right-hand needle. Cut the yarn and thread the cut end through the stitch on the needle. Draw the yarn up firmly to fasten off the last stitch.

On a knit row insert the right-hand needle from left to right through two stitches instead of one, then knit them together as one stitch. This is called knit two together **(k2tog).**

On a purl row insert the right-hand needle from right to left through two stitches instead of one, then purl them together as one stitch. This is called purl two together **(p2tog).**

Increasing

The most usual method of increasing is to work twice into a stitch.

Shaping

A knitted fabric can be shaped to make it narrower or wider by decreasing or increasing the number of stitches on the needle.

Decreasing

The simplest method of decreasing one stitch is to work two stitches together.

On a knit row work into the front and

back of a stitch as follows: knit into the stitch, then before slipping it off the needle, twist the right-hand needle behind the left-hand one and knit again into the back of the loop then slip the original stitch off the left-hand needle.

On a purl row the method is similar. Purl into the front of the stitch, then purl into the back of it before slipping it off the needle.

Making a Stitch

Another form of increasing involves working into the strand between two stitches and is usually called 'make one stitch' **(M1).**

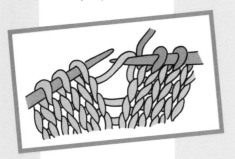

1 Insert the right-hand needle from

front to back under the horizontal strand which runs between the stitches on the needles.

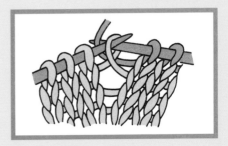

2 Insert the left-hand needle from front to back.

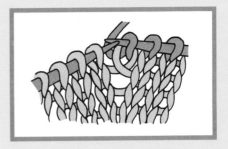

3 Knit or purl through the **back** of the strand twisting the new stitch to prevent the small hole forming.

Joining in New Yarn

Always join in a new ball of yarn at the start of a row wherever possible. If in doubt join in the new ball to avoid the frustration of running out of yarn in the middle of a row and having to unpick the stitches worked.

To make a perfect join at the edge of the work, simply drop the old yarn and start working the row with the new yarn. After a few stitches, tie the old and new ends in a loose knot. The ends can be darned into the seam at a later stage.

Slip Markers

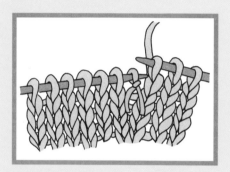

It is sometimes helpful to mark a panel or to separate a motif from the background fabric, or to mark the beginning/end of a round in circular knitting. Make a slip knot in a short length of contrasting yarn and place on needle where required. On the following rows slip the marker from one needle to the other on every row until the pattern is established and the marker is no longer required. For circular knitting, leave the marker in place throughout.

Correcting Dropped Stitches

A stitch dropped a few rows below the work on the needles can be picked up and re-created on each row as long as the work has not progressed too far.

However, if you have continued knitting, the stitches above the dropped stitch will be drawn too tightly across the back of the work to leave enough spare yarn to re-create the lost stitch. In this case it is recommended that you unravel the work to the point where the stitch was dropped and re-knit the unravelled rows.

The easiest method of picking up dropped stitches is to use a crochet hook. Always work with the knit side of the stitch facing you, so you might sometimes have to turn the work over depending on the pattern. Insert the hook into the free stitch from the front. With the hook pointing upwards, catch the first strand of the ladder from above and draw it through the stitch.

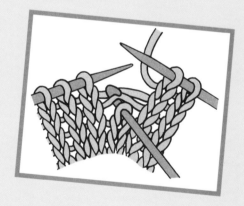

Continue in this way up the ladder until all the strands have been worked, then replace the stitch on the left-hand needle taking care not to twist it. If more than one stitch has dropped, secure the others with a safety pin until you are ready to pick them up.

Working from a Pattern

Before starting to knit your pattern read it through, this will give you an idea of how the pattern is structured. Patterns are written in a language all of their own. Abbreviations are used for many of the repetitive words which occur in the instructions, although not all publications use exactly the same abbreviations, the terminology will soon become familiar.

Abbreviations and Terms

The following terms and abbreviations are used in this publication.

Figures in round brackets ( ) refer to the larger sizes.

Figures or instructions in square brackets [ ] should be repeated as stated after the brackets.

The quantities of yarn are are based on average requirements and are therefore approximate.

Alt = alternate; **beg** = beginning; **cm** = centimetres; **dec** = decrease; **dms** = double moss stitch; **inc** = increase; **ins** = inches; **k** = knit; **p** = purl; **psso** = pass slipped stitch over; **rep** = repeat; **sl** = slip; **st(s)** = stitch(es); **st st** = stocking stitch; **tog** = together; **tbl** = through back of loop; **yb** = yarn back; **yf** = yarn forward; **yfrn** = yarn forward round needle; **yrn** = yarn round needle.

Stitch Charts

Most knitters have already used charts to knit Fairisle or Intarsia patterns. We have given the stitches in this book both written and charted instructions in the hope that you will discover how useful charts can be for stitch patterns. A stitch chart also gives a visual impression of how the finished pattern will appear, enabling instructions for long and complicated patterns to be given in a clear and concise way.

How to Read Charts

Charts are read exactly as the knitting is worked - from the bottom to the top. After the last row has been worked repeat the sequence from the first row.

Each symbol represents an instruction. Symbols have been designed as far as possible to resemble the appearance of the knitting. However it is not always possible to be exact, therefore it is vital that you **always** refer to the detailed description of each symbol.

Before starting to knit look up all the symbols on your chosen chart so that you are familiar with the techniques involved. These are either shown with the pattern as a special abbreviation or with the general abbreviations.

Each square represents a stitch and each horizontal line a row. Place a ruler above the line you are working and work the symbols one by one. If you are new to chart reading you may find it helpful to compare the charted instructions with the written ones.

For knitters who wish to follow the written instructions it is still a good idea to look at the chart before starting, to see what the repeat looks like and how the pattern has been balanced.

Right and Wrong Side Rows

'Right side rows' are rows where the right side of the fabric is facing you when you work and 'wrong side rows' are rows where the wrong side of the fabric is facing you when you work. Row numbers are shown at the side of the charts **at the beginning of the row**.

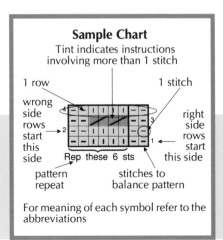

Sample Chart
Tint indicates instructions involving more than 1 stitch

1 row · 1 stitch

wrong side rows start this side

right side rows start this side

Rep these 6 sts

pattern repeat · stitches to balance pattern

For meaning of each symbol refer to the abbreviations

Right side rows are always read from right to left. Wrong side rows are always read from left to right.

Symbols on the charts are shown as they appear from the right side of the work. For example, a horizontal dash stands for a purl 'bump' on the right side regardless of whether it was achieved by purling on a right side row or knitting on a wrong side row.

Note: Symbols are dark on right side rows and light on wrong side rows. Make sure you understand the difference between working similar symbols on a right side row and a wrong side row.

Basic Symbols

☐ **K** knit on right side rows

⊟ **K** knit on wrong side rows

⊟ **P** purl on right side rows

☐ **P** purl on wrong side rows

Panels

A pattern panel is worked across a given number of stitches on a background of a contrasting stitch. To work any of the panels you must cast on enough stitches to work the panel plus the required number of background stitches each side.

All-over Patterns

An all-over pattern is one where the number of stitches given as a multiple is repeated and can be knitted across as narrow or wide a piece of the knitting as required.

43

Pattern Repeats and Multiples

The 'multiple' of each all-over pattern is given with each set of instructions, for example:- **'Multiple of 7 sts + 4'.** This means that you can cast on any number of stitches which is a multiple of 7 plus 4 stitches; for instance 14 + 4 sts, 21 + 4 sts, 28 + 4 sts etc.

In the written instructions the 7 stitches are shown in parentheses or brackets or follow an asterisk (shown as *), and these stitches are repeated across the row the required number of times. In charted instructions the multiple is indicated by a bracket at the bottom of the chart and heavier vertical lines. The extra stitches not included in the multiple are there to 'balance' the row or make it symmetrical and are only worked once.

Tension or Gauge

Knitting tension or gauge refers to the number of stitches and rows in a given area. You have to produce fabric with the same number of stitches and rows as given in the tension paragraph so that you obtain the correct measurements for the garment you intend to knit.

The needle size indicated in the pattern is the one which **most** knitters will use to achieve this tension, but it is the tension that is important, not the needle size.

The way to ensure that you do achieve a correct tension is to work a tension sample or swatch before starting the main part of the knitting.

Making a Tension Swatch

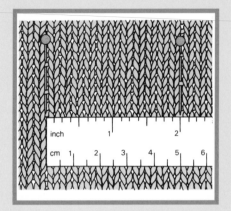

1 The instructions given in the tension paragraph of a pattern will be either over stocking stitch or the pattern stitch used for the garment. Cast on the correct multiple of stitches to be able to work the pattern for a swatch at least 12 cm [5 ins] in width. Work in the required pattern until the piece measures approximately 12 cm [5 ins], then break the yarn, thread it through the stitches and slip them off the needle. Do not cast off or measure the swatch while still on the needle as this could distort the stitches.

2 First measure the stitch tension across the centre of the swatch by counting the number of stitches stated in the pattern's recommended tension. Mark either end with pins. If your tension is correct the measurement between the pins should be the same as that stated in the pattern.

If the measurement is more, then your knitting is too loose, try making another swatch using smaller needles. If the measurement is less than required try making another swatch using larger needles.

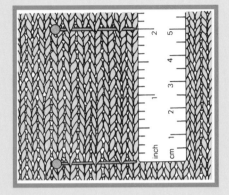

3 For the row tension count the number of rows recommended in the pattern vertically down the centre of the fabric avoiding the rows at the edges of the swatch. Mark with pins at each end and then check the distance between them. Once the stitch tension is right, the row tension is most likely to be correct. Any slight inaccuracies could be overlooked as the lengthwise proportions of a garment are **usually** given as a measurement.

Measuring a Garment

To measure a piece of knitting while it is in progress, spread the work out flat on a table. Never stretch the knitting and always ensure that the width measurement is correct before measuring the length. Unless otherwise stated, always measure widths horizontally and lengths vertically - never diagonally.

Finishing

The importance of the finishing stages of a garment should never be overlooked. Too often a garment can be spoilt by rushing the final stages, and the time and effort taken to knit it is wasted if the end result is unsatisfactory. A better appearance can be gained by pressing the separate pieces before sewing them together.

Always check the ball band for information on whether or not the yarn should be pressed - this should also tell you the heat setting of the iron and whether to use a dry or damp cloth.

Some types of knitting or parts of a garment are best left unpressed. Pressing may flatten the texture and blur the details, and can make the ribbing lose its elasticity.

If in any doubt about pressing, always try pressing the tension piece first to avoid spoiling the actual garment.

Pressing

The characteristics of yarns vary greatly and information for individual yarns is usually given on the ball band. If none is available use the following as a general guide.

Wool, cotton, linen and other natural yarns - press work on wrong side using hot iron and a damp cloth avoiding all ribbing.

Synthetics - press lightly on the wrong side using a **cool** iron and a dry cloth, avoiding all ribbing.

Picking up Stitches

Once the main body of the knitting is complete it is sometimes necessary to add an edging or border. These can be knitted separately and sewn on, but it is quicker and easier to pick up the stitches along the edges and knit directly into these.

It is important that the stitches are divided equally along the length of the fabric, and also that they are picked up **either** through a whole stitch **or** half a stitch throughout to ensure an even line along the edge.

To calculate how to pick up the stitches, lay the edge to be used straight and measure its length. Place a pin at the halfway point at right angles to the edge, then halve these distances again and again, so that the length is divided into eighths. Divide the given number of stitches by eight and pick up approximately this number in each section, check that the total number of stitches has been picked up at the end.

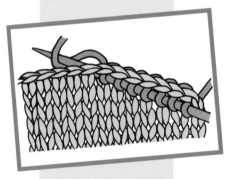

To pick stitches up along a cast-on/cast-off edge have the right side of the work facing you and insert the point of the right-hand needle from front to back under **both** loops of the cast on or cast off edge of first stitch, wind the yarn around the needle as though knitting a stitch and draw a loop through to form a new stitch on the needle. Continue in this way along the edge as required.

When picking up stitches along a side edge insert the point of the right-hand needle from front to back between the first and second stitch of the first row, a whole stitch in from edge. Alternatively, if the yarn is very thick work through the centre of the edge stitch, thus taking in only half a stitch.

Sewing Up

Use a blunt-ended needle and the yarn you have been knitting with for the seams unless it is thick or textured, then use a finer, toning coloured yarn.

Mattress Stitch Seam

1 With the right side facing you, lay the two pieces to be joined flat and edge to edge. Insert the needle between the edge stitch and the second stitch on the first row. Pass the needle under two rows, then bring it back through to the front.

2 Return to the opposite side and, working under **two** rows at a time throughout, repeat this zigzag action always taking the needle under the strands that correspond exactly to the other side, and going into the hole that the last stitch on that side came out of, taking care not to miss any rows.

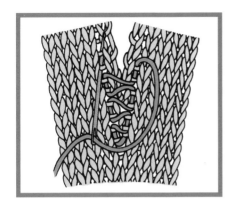

The secret of good mattress stitching is to keep the seam elastic without allowing it to stretch too much. The best way to do this is to work loosely for approximately 5 cm [2 ins] then pull the thread very firmly so that the stitches are held together quite tightly. Now stretch the seam slightly to give the required amount of elasticity, then continue with the seam.

When the purl side of the fabric is the right side, you may find that you achieve a better effect by working under **one** row at a time rather than the two rows as described above.

When joining two ribbed sections together, it is best to take in only half a stitch on either side, so that when the pieces are drawn together one complete knit stitch is formed.

Grafting

Grafting invisibly joins two pieces of knitting. The edges are not cast off and the stitches can either be on or off the needles.

With right sides facing lay the pieces to be joined close together, with the stitches on each piece corresponding to those opposite.

1 Beginning on the right-hand side, bring the needle up through the first stitch of the lower piece from back to front, then through the first stitch of the upper piece from back to front. Bring it down through the first stitch of the lower piece from front to back and up again through the next stitch to the left from back to front.

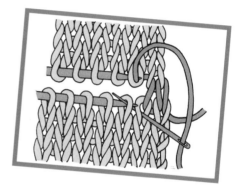

2 *On the upper piece, pass the needle down from front to back through the same stitch it came up through before and bring it up from back to front through the next stitch to the left. If working with stitches still on the needles slip them off one by one as they are secured.

3 On the lower piece, take the needle down from front to back through the stitch it came up through before and bring it up through the next stitch to the left from back to front.

Repeat from * to the end, keeping the tension the same as the knitted fabric.

Top of the Class

Hints and tips to help and improve your knitting.

If you are using fluffy yarns you may find that they 'shed', or that the fibres of one colour become entangled with another. Keep each colour in a separate plastic bag to avoid this, secured loosely with an elastic band. This also helps to keep light colours clean.

If you want to work out your own Intarsia or motif pattern or adapt embroidery charts, this can be done on graph paper. However, stitches are not square and if squared graph paper is used, the pattern will appear wider and shorter on the knitted piece. Graph paper in the correct proportions can now be obtained from specialist knitting shops specifically for this purpose.

When joining in a new colour for any type of knitting, always leave a long enough end for darning in.

As colour choice is so personal, do experiment yourself with colour combinations. A design knitted in bold contrast colours will look entirely different if soft muted colours are used. Why not try making use of a pleasing colour combinations already in existance? A favourite scarf, toy, rug or set of curtains can all provide inspiration. Having chosen a design it is well worth knitting samples in several colour combinations before commencing a garment.

Yarn equivalent table

UK	Double Knitting
Australia	8 ply
New Zealand	Doubleknit
North America	Sports Weight
South Africa	Double Knitting